Insights

Tantric Buddhist
Reflections on Life

Rama – Dr. Frederick Lenz

INSIGHTS:
TANTRIC BUDDHIST REFLECTIONS ON LIFE
by Rama – Dr. Frederick Lenz

Published by
InterGlobal Seminars, Inc.
New York, New York

First Edition
Printed in the United States of America
on acid-free paper

Library of Congress Catalog Card No. 94-77447
ISBN 0-9642196-7-0

Table of Contents

Enlightenment...3

Meditation...4

Karma...6

Fate...8

Freedom...9

Self-Knowledge...10

Death...11

Love...12

The Inner Buddha...13

Dharma...14

Knowing...16

Others...18

Illusions...19

Mortality...20

Happiness...21

Sex...22

Self-Acceptance...23

Power...24

Immortality...25

Respect...26

Feelings...27

Loneliness...28

Friendship...29

Fears...30

Being and Nonbeing...32

Fire!...34

The Buddhist Order...35

Willpower...38

Opportunities...39

Yoga...40

God...41

Evil...42

Running Away...43

Perfection...44

More Fun!...45

Thinking...46

Intuition...47

Oblivion...48

Color Portraits...49

Intent...50

Honesty...52

Peak Experiences...53

Be Drunken...54

Fluidity...55

Forgiveness...56

Dying...57

Normality...58

Advice...59

Enlightened Masters...60

Effort...61

Simplify...62

Readiness...63

Trust...65

Trouble...66

Puzzles...67

Three Things...68

Beyond...69

Give It Up!...70

Completion...71

Enlightenment

Beyond the surface of your life there is enlightenment,
In all of its joyous radiant perfection.
When, sitting absorbed in meditation, your thoughts
Become quiet and your emotions are still,
Your mind floods with light and the world becomes God.

> Enlightenment is the perfect awareness of life
> Without any mental modifications.
> It is transparent existence:
> To experience enlightenment, to merge
> Your mind with the essence of the cosmos,
> Is to become ecstasy without beginning or end.

Enlightenment is beyond human understanding:
From the shores of this world, human life appears
To be an endless tide of happy and unhappy
Events, feelings and circumstances;
But when viewed through the eyes of enlightenment
There is no pleasure, pain, loss or gain,
No illusion or reality, or even incarnation.
There is only perfectly intelligent
Immortal Light!

Meditation

Meditation is the bridge between this
And all other levels of consciousness;
Practicing meditation makes you aware of
Your eternally enlightened nature.

Sit in meditation until
Your mind becomes empty;
Sit in meditation without thought
And the winds of consciousness will
Blow visions of radiant worlds of light
Before your inner eyes.

By practicing meditation you will gradually
Change the limited view that you have of yourself;
This misunderstanding of who and what you are
Is the cause of all of your pain.

Your personality identifies itself
With your physical body:
It believes that it
Came into existence at the
Time of your physical birth,
And that it will cease to exist
At the time of your physical death.
Your personality doesn't realize that beneath
The transient surface of your physical body,
You have another body that is made up of eternal
Light that cannot be born and cannot die!
It is made up of the ecstatic everythingness
And the eternal nothingness of nirvana!

By practicing meditation you will come to see
That the true nature of the real you,
The body of light,
Is everlasting bliss!
So push past sorrow and pain
Because within you is ecstatic
Life everlasting!

Karma

When you change your awareness,
You change your karma.

Karma is your current awareness:
It is the level of consciousness
That you are presently experiencing,
Right here and now!

The karma of your current awareness has
Been shaped by the experiences that you have
Had in this and in all of your other lifetimes.

If you would like to improve your karma,
If you would like to experience deeper
Levels of happiness and ecstasy,
Then you must expand your
Awareness into light!

Changing your karma means letting go
Of your current personality
And upgrading it to a more
Lucid personality which
Is brighter and deeper
Than the personality
You now have.

You need to start,
Organize,
Participate in,
And win
A revolution
Within your own mind,
Which will oust the despotic
Dictator "Ego!"

Meditate upon the all perfect
Light within your own mind!
Do this repeatedly and the radiant
Bodhisattvas of Wisdom and Laughter
Will visit you and change your karma forever!

Fate

There is no such thing as fate.
To say that there is fate is to suggest that
Everything in your life is predestined.
No way!

Buddhism is based upon the principle of free will:
With our free will we can gradually make changes in
Our karmic patterns and create new and more
Beautiful moments in our lives.

If we maximize our free will we can even
Come to know nirvana,
Which is beyond
The
Mind's
Knowing
And any
Other type
Of limitation!

Freedom

Freedom is the ability to dream:
To be able to roam endlessly through
The multifaceted mind of eternity.

Beyond this thin surface of existence
That we call life, is perennial awareness:
A field of both light and dark dreams.

Think it over.
Beyond this moment are all
Other possible moments,
Existing forever like dark stars in
A white night sky.
There is no beginning or ending to any of this,
It all goes on, as do we, forever.

Freedom is the ability to dream new dreams,
As you roam happily through the mind of God;
Your current self is one of those dreams,
As are all of your experiences in each new life.

To free your mind from the dreams of self
And to explore enlightened levels of
Perception is to practice yoga;
All that is required is a yen to travel
Through that hidden country that we call nirvana.

Self-Knowledge

Self-knowledge is happiness.
It's really that simple.
Self-knowledge exists beyond the pains, fears,
Passions, loves, hates, depressions, triumphs,
Defeats and other ranges of human experience.
It is like an oasis in the midst of a desert;
The hot pains of life's journey are quickly
Forgotten amid the life-quenching happiness
That you find there.

As long as you abide in self-knowledge you will be
Sheltered from the hot burning pains of life;
But if you leave self-knowledge you will
Become a desert traveller again,
Joining a caravan that journeys through the
Intense heat, cold, pleasure and pain of
Life's experiences — until one day,
Your caravan will find the oasis of
Self-knowledge again.

Death

Death is an inevitable journey
That we all must take.
At first we watch others we know go on ahead of us,
Until, quite unexpectedly, it is our turn to go.
On an unknown day or night we will be summoned
To journey forward into yet another life.

Death is not an ending — so don't be afraid of it!
It is only a punctuation mark in the endless
Saga of our lives.
Cast your mind backward and recall
The tens of thousands of your past lives.
Cast your mind forward and feel your future lives,
The tens of thousands that are yet to be.
Now concentrate upon this moment,
In this lifetime, and see how fully you can live it!

You've died many times before and,
To be honest with you,
You don't look any the worse for it —
So why fear death anyway?

Love

Throw away your life,
So that you can find it again!
Unless what you are doing today is
Leading you to much greater happiness,
Whatever you are doing is a waste of your time!

What good are families, friends, possessions and
The trivial pursuits of human life unless they
Free you from who you are now? Instead just
Throw them all away and seek enlightenment
In whatever life makes available to you.
Stop kidding yourself. If your life is
Not filled with more love every day,
It's time to throw away your life,
So that you can find it again!

The Inner Buddha

All praise to the inner Buddha!
The enlightened part of our nature!
It is the wisdom of existence in incarnate form!
And it deserves your immediate attention!

Forget about your life.
It has no meaning or purpose unless you are
Seeking enlightenment!

Could you be stupid enough to believe in the
Hollow dreams of unhappy humanity?
What they are selling out there
Is definitely not worth buying;
It only leads to disappointment and endless pain.

Learn to meditate and seek an enlightened master,
One who has awakened from the dreams of life.
Then be with your master and do as he says.
Learn from him, meditate upon him,
And overcome yourself.
Find the inner Buddha and you will be free!

Dharma

In every age it is proclaimed
By enlightened teachers!
It is said in different languages
In different ways at different times!
But it is, in essence, always the same —
It is the Dharma, the true reason for living
And being. It is as constant as change for the
Living, and as certain as rebirth for the dying.

What is the Dharma?
It is this:
We are all drowning in the ocean of life,
We are all drowning in the ocean of death,
The wheel of creation spins us
Ceaselessly
From
Incarnation
To
Incarnation.
We are all drowning in the ocean of existence.

And yet there are a few who are immune
To all of this drowning,
To all of this constant living and dying.
They swim in the oceans of life and death unaffected
By the ceaseless agony and ecstasy of incarnation,
By all of this drowning;
For they are enlightened,
Enlightenment in incarnate form,
And they sing hymns to the drowning,
Chants to take away our fears.
And if we reach out and call to them
To save us from all of this living and dying,
They laugh at us and at our tears
And tell us that we are already saved,
Saved by our drowning,
By our living and dying,
In this ocean of life,
In this ocean of death.

Knowing

There are steps to knowing,
To becoming aware of what lies beyond all of this.
The first step is a longing — for another time,
Another place and another condition,
That is more perfect and free.

The second step is the search for the method
Of becoming free.
This is the fun part!
You must find out how to meditate and
What to meditate upon.
You must search for your teacher
And find a way to be accepted by him.
To do this you must be inventive, creative
And attached to nothing at all except these goals.

If you must travel the world over in search — you must;
If you must read every book about meditation until you
Have read and reread them all many times — you must;
If you must listen to hundreds of pompous teachers
Who are filled up only with their own egos — you must.
You must listen to them,
Until you find the one that glows with the
Golden light of enlightenment.

The third part is what I call the discipline of
Enlightenment. It is really the best part.
You must overcome your ego and finally put it to rest.
You must practice your meditation until it is perfect.
You must listen to your teacher until you can hear
Nothing else: Not what you want to hear, not
Your version of what he is saying,
But exactly what he has said!

The last part is to be alone.
This is the test.
You can meditate perfectly.
You have overcome ego.
You have become a reflection of your teacher's mind,
The mind and the heart of enlightenment.
Now you must face aloneness,
The immensity of all being,
Because you have learned that emptiness and fullness
Are as transient as the spring flowers,
As youth, and as promises
Made in the heat of passion.

My personal advice,
When you reach this stage,
Is to face the immensity of life,
All of the teeming
Worlds of brightness
That stretch out into infinity,
With a smile.

Others

Everyone's quest is the same,
To find one's own perfection.
That is really all that any one of us is seeking.

Each being comes out of nirvana wanting everything;
Seeking to know and experience all possibilities.
Like birds who make their nests out of whatever life
Affords them, each of us makes the mandala of our
Current incarnation out of whatever we are drawn to.

From lifetime to lifetime we are drawn back
To familiar persons, places and things.
The enlightened call this "sameness,"
A feeling of pleasure in internal
And external surroundings
That are familiar to us.

When beings agree upon their illusions,
They feel close to each other.
When they no longer share the same illusions,
They drift apart,
Each seeking a separate reality.

Illusions — the things that we are attracted to, want,
Believe in, or wish to have happen to us — create our
Associations. They join us for a time
In the ocean of life
To others, until
One day we
Are free.

Illusions

The enlightened ones stand upon a threshold
Of endless mind from which they can see
In the distance and close at hand the
Endless illusions of eternity.

Life is walking on a beach and watching the waves
That are perpetually moving forward towards you,
Staring out at the edge of the blue horizon,
Your body buffeted by a strong sea breeze,
Watching the seagulls rising and falling in the sky,
This perception of infinity.

Why is all of this?
What is all of this?
Does life have a beginning and an end?
Is there a purpose or meaning?

The seagulls turn and dive in the wind,
Searching for their purpose,
And at night they sleep in their nests,
And dream of fish
And of flying
In the wind.

Mortality

The lessons of life are plain, simple and few:
Don't get caught in the rain unless you
Want to get wet;
Try to avoid people, places and experiences that
Don't make you smile;
Never count on anyone except yourself;
And never ever forget that you are
Already dead in the future.

Mortality, this necessity of living and dying,
Is the core of existence.
It is the lesson you have incarnated to learn:
To be who you are now, and then not to be,
To accept this gratefully and without despair,
Neither to run away from nor towards life,
But to view your life with eyes
Wide open to all that you see,
To bear witness without condemnation, despair,
Hate or recrimination,
To simply watch the passing of life as
A newborn child does, eyes wide open to eternity.

Happiness

Happiness comes from loving something or someone.
This is the wisdom of the enlightened!
Happiness ends when you stop loving,
And start hating the things and people that you loved.

Sex

Sex is life:
The act of creation in pleasure,
The loss of oneself in another,
The coming together of opposites
In a temporary union of yin and yang
That creates something other than either.

What is life if not this?

Self-Acceptance

To accept your physical body,
This transient home of the soul,
As a perfect mandala of enlightenment, is wisdom.
To see your physical body and its processes
As anything less than enlightenment is a mistake.

I know that there are many spiritual traditions
That disagree with me;
According to them your physical body is corrupt.

I don't really care.
Because to criticize the physical body is to
Criticize the designs and the designer of creation.
It is a sign of spiritual immaturity and weakness.
Only a strong, mature and wise person can
Embrace all of existence as God.

To do this you must see beyond the surface of life
And know its deeper reality.
Those who reject the physical and praise the spiritual
Have not yet passed the universe's course in
Self-acceptance.

Power

Power is conscious awareness.
The most powerful are those who are consciously
Aware of the limitless possibilities of incarnation.

Power involves the ability to both take and give life.
The universe is that which is most powerful,
And what does it do?
It both takes and gives life constantly.

Some think that the taking of life is the ultimate
Expression of power.
And then there are those who profess that giving and
Creating life is even more powerful.
Personally I don't really see a difference,
Since the taking and the giving of life require
Equal acts of will.

To be truly powerful, one must be a conduit of
Both of these sides of the universe,
And this requires full conscious awareness,
Not of killing or of creating,
But of the forces behind these twin actions.
Get a clue!

Immortality

Immortality is all around you,
Can you see it?
Immortality is life's music,
Can you hear it?
Immortality is love,
Can you feel it?
Immortality is life,
Can you taste it?
Immortality is the scent of life,
Can you smell it?
Immortality is in your thoughts,
Can you sense it?
Immortality is who you are,
The bright being whose awareness
Holds all of this together,
And without whose life
None of this would be.

Respect

Enlightenment comes to those who respect life,
To those who gently and patiently
Probe its mysteries.

To feel beyond feeling,
Touch beyond touching,
Know beyond knowing,
And be beyond being,
Is to respect life.

Feelings

Feelings come with a body, mind and spirit.
They are not as important as they might seem and
Yet they are the very substance of our lives.

When your feelings are painful, it is best to
Disregard them.
When your feelings are pleasurable, it is best to
Enjoy them.
To experience enlightenment, you must
Learn to rise above them!

Loneliness

Loneliness is the best friend of the spiritual seeker.
In loneliness we can feel the perfect immensity and
Splendor of all of the endless universes within us.
Loneliness purifies the spirit and for this reason,
At most times, I choose to be alone.

Loneliness is the soul's search for God.
It is your spirit's celebration of itself!
It is not a sad, bad or unhappy thing.
It is your soul's song of its
Experiences in existence.

Friendship

Make friends with the universe today!
The universe is your true friend:
Eventually everyone and everything else leaves you;
Only the universe accompanies you on your endless
Journey through timeless existence.

The universe is warm and happy as a puppy,
But you must get past your fears to know this.

In deep meditation, you can feel the all perfect
Light of enlightenment shining through all things;
This is the friendship of the universe extending
Itself to you.

Fears

What are you afraid of?
There is only life.

Fears are like comets:
They follow erratic yet regular orbits.
You will notice that the same fears return to you
At different times and in different places
Concerning the same things,
Again and again.

Your fears define your life.
They won't go away; they will just continue their orbit
Until it is time for them to return to you again.

The only way to eliminate your fears is to
Become someone else!
The reason is simple:
Your fears know you.
They have a well-developed sense
Of who you are.
They know what you like,
What you don't like,
And most importantly,
They know what makes you reach out to them.

The antidote to your fears, of course, is courage;
The courage to change who you are.
When you become someone other than who you have been,
Your fears become confused because they
Can't recognize you.
They zip around searching for you for a time and then
They simply up and leave, never to return again!

The act of courage necessary to change
Your identity is to meditate deeply.
When you meditate deeply, you
Bring your mind into light.
Then the person who you
Have been dissolves
In the clear light
Of reality.
It's that
Simple!

Being and Nonbeing

Between here and there,
Time and space,
Man and woman,
Yin and yang,
Brightness and darkness,
And just about anything else
You can think of, there is
Being and nonbeing.

What is being?
Being is consciousness.
Or more precisely, to be conscious.
And to be even more precise, who is conscious.
And to hassle the details, being is
Who is conscious and what they are conscious of.

Nonbeing is easier:
Nonbeing is unconsciousness.

In your quest for enlightenment you will learn
A great deal about being and nonbeing,
Because enlightenment is neither.
Enlightenment is like a highway that can
Only be reached by journeying down other roads
That lead to it.
There are many different roads that you can take in
Life, and most of them don't lead to enlightenment.
But being and nonbeing, even though they have nothing
Directly to do with enlightenment,
Will lead you there.

Some hints from someone (that's me) who has travelled
Down the bumpy roads that lead to enlightenment and
Quite a few of the roads that don't:

To find the road of being you must:

First!   Love someone or something more than
You love yourself.

Second!   Take chances constantly.

Third!   Stop taking yourself so seriously.

Fourth!   Start taking others more seriously.

Fifth!   Never give up hope.

Sixth!   Meditate more deeply today than you ever have.

Seventh!   Learn to dance.

Eighth!   Feel the pain of the world and be happy
Anyway.

Ninth!   Let go and let eternity do with you what it
Will.

Tenth!   Look beyond all of this and know the truth.

To find the road of nonbeing you must
Simply overcome yourself.

Fire!

Buddhism teaches that the world is on fire!
We are all living in a burning house,
But like a drugged person who sits in a
House that is on fire and is oblivious
To the peril,
We live our lives unaware of the consequences
Of our actions — the effects they will produce
In terms of the experiences that we will have
Both later in this incarnation and in our
Future lives.

Most people think that an enlightened Buddhist
Teacher is a fireman;
His job is to put the fire out so that
You can live in your home safely.
But seeker beware!
A fully enlightened Buddhist teacher is an
Arsonist!
His job is to set your spirit on fire!
By feeding the flames of your soul with love.

The Buddhist Order

Buddhism is the way of yoga,
It is a quiet way of living your life,
It is meditation,
Ethics,
Cosmology,
The pathway to enlightenment
And mystical practices.

The Buddhist Order is open to anyone;
You can join!
But first you must be initiated by a
Senior member of the Order.

I would be glad to initiate you
And put you
"On the path,"
As we say in Buddhism;
The pathway to enlightenment, that is.

But before I initiate you I must ask you several
Questions. Don't be afraid. I have put the answers
Underneath the questions, just in case you have
Forgotten them since your last incarnation.

1. Do you know what Buddhism is?
  Buddhism is the search for bodhi — enlightenment.
  All people who seek enlightenment are Buddhists,
  Whether they realize it or not.

2. Do you know what enlightenment is?
   (Trick question, don't fall for it.)
   No one knows what enlightenment is,
   Including incarnate Buddhas.
   The correct answer is: "No, I don't.
   Enlightenment is beyond the mind's
   Knowing."

3. What is the cause of pain?
   Cable TV.

4. Funny. What is the real cause of pain?
   Attachment to desires.
   (This is a great answer!
   The usual answer is "attachment."
   But when you answer "attachment to desires" you
   Indicate by your answer that you have a much more
   Subtle grasp of the teachings of Buddhism than
   The average applicant has.)

5. What are the Four Noble Truths?
   A rap group.
   (Very funny. Have you thought about going on
   Star Search? *Try again.)*

6. What are the Four Noble Truths?
   1. The life of an unenlightened person is filled
   With suffering.

2. *The cause of suffering*
   Is a lack of enlightenment, which is caused
   By a person's attachment to desires
   And aversion to suffering.
3. *There is a way to reach enlightenment*
   And get beyond suffering.
4. *Meditation is the pathway to enlightenment.*

7. In a Zen sense, what is illusion, and what is truth?
   Truth is who you see in the mirror.
   Illusion is who you see in the mirror.

Since you now know all of the answers, I will
Initiate you as a member of the Order and put you
On
The path.
There, it's done.

Just one more question before you start your
Journey — from Rama — who has put countless seekers
Of enlightenment on the path
Over the course of countless lifetimes:

8. What is the most important thing to remember now
   That you are a member of the Order and have been
   Put on the path?
   Stay on the path.

Willpower

Willpower is the ability to make things happen.
All kinds of things.
It is also the ability to make things not happen.
All kinds of things.
Willpower is developed over the course of time,
Through the practice of concentration.
It is like developing a muscle;
You must use your muscle in order to develop it.

Opportunities

A new opportunity exists in every second!
I'm not being glib. It's true.
Every second you have the opportunity to
Love instead of hate,
To be positive instead of negative,
To smile instead of frown,
To believe instead of disbelieve.

By loving, being positive, smiling and believing
On a second-to-second basis, no matter what is
Happening externally or internally to you,
You become superior to fate.

Yoga

Your mind is a complicated thing;
It is made up of countless layers.
Underneath all of those layers is nirvana,
Bright, shining, perfect and beyond knowing.

The journey of life is within:
All of the experiences we pass through are really
Only reflections of our different mental states.

Enlightenment, the experience of nirvana,
Is at the center of our being.
It is like the earth's molten core,
Unseen but all powerful.

The surface of your mind is made up of different
Dimensions.
Yoga is a way of moving through these dimensions
Of mind and reaching the molten core of light
Within you.

When the surface, self-conscious awareness of your
Mind is conjoined with nirvana,
Self-knowledge is attained.

God

God is within your mind.
God is within all things.
As a matter of fact,
There is nothing that is not God.

What is evil?
There is no such thing.
In Buddhism we don't recognize evil and
Therefore we don't give it any power over us.

Running Away

Running away is an exercise in futility.
What are you running away from?
Who are you running away from?
Since you exist in all things
And in all places,
You are only running
Away from yourself.

Instead of running away, try running to.
Run to happiness,
Run to self-knowledge,
Run to ecstasy,
Run to peace and stillness,
Run to humor,
Run to oblivion.

Remember: Wherever you go, there you are!

Perfection

The mind of the Buddha is perfect
Because it is empty and yet
It contains all things.

More Fun!

Why aren't you having more fun with
The moments of your life?
Since they won't come again
It seems like a waste of time not to enjoy them!

Maybe this is why you aren't having more fun;
Perhaps you feel that you have so much
Time at your disposal that you can waste
As much of it as you like.

Look around you.
Everyone and everything dies here.
There are no survivors on the prison ship earth!
Since the moment of your death is uncertain,
And usually comes when you are
Least prepared for it,
Why don't you stop wasting your time and
Start having more fun with the moments of your life
Right now?

Thinking

Thinking is usually a waste of time and energy,
Since thinking is essentially a rehashing of
What we already know.
As a matter of fact, thinking is an easy way
To confuse yourself.
The more you think, the less you know.

Intuition

Intuition is a lightning flash of understanding,
A momentless moment of self-reflection
In which you come to understand all things.
Meditation, the suspension of thought,
Clears the air for intuition,
Which will come to you soon.
Be patient,
Wait,
Keep meditating.

Oblivion

We all seek oblivion:
As the sperm seeks the egg,
As the newborn seeks the breast,
As life seeks death,
And as death seeks rebirth.

The spirit seeks oblivion:
To dissolve in the white light of eternity,
To lose and find itself endlessly in
Oceans of shifting and shimmering light.

Color Portraits

Your life is a scrapbook that is made up of
Color portraits.
All the moments of your current and past lives
Have been recorded
And preserved as color portraits,
For you to look back upon in your future lives.

In your next life how will all of these moments look?
Were you brave or were you timid?
Did you strive to develop your higher self,
Or did you just hang out?
Someday you will open the scrapbook of your
Past lives and turn to the page that you are
Living right now.
How will it look to you then?
Will you laugh, cry or be bored,
As you view these color portraits,
These fleeting moments of your life?

Intent

In High Buddhist talk we use the word "intent"
To describe a person's reasons for doing and being.
We feel that nothing creates happiness or
Unhappiness as strongly as intent does.

Intent is our bottom-line motivation.
When all of the props are removed and the
Makeup is off, we are left alone with our intent.

We are all aware of our real intent;
You may fool others by masking your intent,
But you can't fool your own karma.

Why do you suffer so much?
It is because your intent is not in harmony with
Your soul.
Until you correct the discrepancy between your mind's
Intent and your soul's proclivity for light,
You will never be at peace with yourself.

And remember, your life is not a sitcom on TV.
A happy ending is not built into the script of
Your life, unless you write it in yourself by
Having correct intent.

What is correct intent?
From a Buddhist point of view, correct intent is to
Seek happiness without intentionally doing harm
To others.
Incorrect intent is to seek happiness for yourself
By ripping other people off.
Exceptional intent is to seek happiness for yourself by
Spreading light and empowering others.

No one said that you had to be a saint to be happy,
And being a saint may not be as straightlaced
An affair as you might think it is.
All that matters is to realize
That the only person you are
Really going to hurt in
The end is yourself.
So why don't you
Clean up your
Act and be
Happy?

Honesty

Honesty, like ice cream, comes in different flavors:
There is day-to-day honesty,
Lying-to-yourself honesty,
Shining-everyone-else-on honesty,
Shining-yourself-on honesty,
"I'm sorry, I'll never do it again" honesty,
"I'll start my diet tomorrow" honesty,
And the flavor-of-the-month honesty:
"I really didn't enjoy doing that,"
When in fact you know that you did!

Then there is Buddhist honesty:
Realizing that you are imperfect,
Not making a big deal about it,
Striving to be more perfect
Because it feels better to,
Not lying to yourself, ever,
Not lying to others unless it is
In their best interest,
And simply being who you are,
In spite of all outer and internal
Opposition!

Buddhist honesty clarifies your life.

Peak Experiences

You can spend your time in the
Valleys of life,
Or you can have peak experiences!

Peak experiences occur when the kundalini
Is released and it flows up your spine.
Meditation creates peak experiences,
And so do a surprising number of other pursuits.
The more something excites you, the more
Kundalini is released.
The greater the amount of kundalini released,
The higher your peak experience will be.
So interface with that which excites you in life,
And don't forget to meditate!

Be Drunken

Be drunken on life!
Meditate and lose all sensibility.
This is the essence of all spiritual practice.
This is the point of all Tantric Yogic teachings.

Be drunken on life!
Allow meditation to intoxicate you completely.
Only when you are completely intoxicated with life
Will you begin to know what the ultimate reality is!

Be drunken on life!
Drink in the ecstasy of meditation until you
Can drink no more!
Sobriety and self-discovery have nothing in common so
Be drunken!

Fluidity

Buddhist Yoga teaches us to be fluid,
To go with the flow of life.
When you think of yourself as something solid
Like ice, then it's hard to be fluid.
When you melt yourself with the
Heat of meditation,
Then fluidity comes naturally.
You can always become whoever you need to be,
And fit into whatever situation that arises.

Some might view this as being inconsistent,
But from a Buddhist point of view it is simply
A small but important matter of being polite.

Forgiveness

Forgiveness is the ultimate revenge.

Dying

Dying is easy;
It's living that's difficult.

Normality

Normality does not create enlightenment;
If you want to become enlightened
You must go to extremes!
You must be extremely centered,
Extremely optimistic,
Extremely enthusiastic,
And extremely faithful
To your practice of Buddhist Yoga.

Advice

The best advice is usually ignored,
So I make it a point never to give
My students advice.
Instead I teach them intent and method.
I save the advice for myself.
I listen
Because many, many lifetimes of practicing yoga
Have taught me to hassle the details;
Taking advice from an enlightened Buddhist Master
And acting upon it with a smile
Is hassling the details.

Enlightened Masters

Enlightened Buddhist Masters are hard to work with
Because they are:
Touchy,
Critical,
Changeable,
Aloof,
Overly friendly,
Too optimistic,
Too pessimistic,
Too realistic,
Never tell you what you want to hear,
Never appreciate your efforts,
Always point out your weak spots,
Are unattached to everyone and everything,
Don't grant you your every wish,
Make fun of you on a regular basis,
Are always on time even when they are late,
Have power but are controlled,
Are infinitely more happy than you are,
Are empty,
Are able to do things you can't,
Are above desire and aversion,
Always do what is spiritually correct,
Pay no attention to your preconceived
Notions of what they should be like or
How they should act,
Turn gold when they meditate,
Don't care about morality or immorality,
Will do anything to alleviate the spiritual
Suffering of another,
Love God beyond comprehension,
Have passed beyond the boundaries of human reason,
And are always able to find a parking space
Quickly and without apparent effort.

Effort

Give up trying so hard,
And try harder!
The things in your life
That seem so important
To you right now, aren't;
The things in your life
That seem so unimportant
To you right now, are!

Stop trying to correct the world
And instead correct yourself;
This will make you happier
And you will have
More friends.

Start filling your mind with light
By focusing more on nirvana
And less on yourself.

What is nirvana?
That which is the highest,
Brightest, and purest of all.
It is the essence of all things
Both visible and invisible.

In meditation,
Quiet your mind
Until there is no thought.
In meditation,
Quiet your mind
Until there is no self.
In meditation,
Quiet your mind
Until there is no mind.
This is nirvana!

Simplify

Simplify your life.
It's really that simple!
Simplify your life by removing the thoughts
From your mind that cause you so much pain.
Simplify your life by removing the
Fears and doubts from your mind
That cause you so much pain.
Simplify your life until
Only happiness remains!

Readiness

Always be prepared!
Anything can and will happen
When you least expect it!

Did you expect to be born when you were?
Did you expect to be who you have become?
Do you know what is going to happen to you next?

Be ready for anything and everything
Because anything and everything is exactly
What happens to you at any given moment.

The best way to be ready is to be strong,
Hopeful, optimistic, realistic,
Flexible and funny.

Meditation and mindfulness will make you ready.
Studying with the enlightened will
Sharpen your readiness!

Spending time alone in nature
And reflecting upon the
Perfection within all
Things will finish
The job!

Be ready at all times!
Exercise your mind and body,
Laugh and love,
And respect
The Dharma.

Be kind when you can be,
Understanding when you can't,
And joyful under all circumstances.
Then you will always be ready!
Ready to experience the
Beauty and the
Perfection of
All.

Trust

Trust is perhaps the most difficult thing
To achieve, since everyone tells you lies.
Even your own thoughts and perceptions can
Tell you lies. How, then, can you trust?
Who can you trust? What can you trust?

I have learned a Buddhist secret about
Trusting that I will share with you.
It goes something like this:
Trust innocence, nothing else.
And what is innocence,
You might ask?
Innocence is the lack of
Self-consciousness
In all things;
It is beyond desire
And aversion,
It is the enlightened
Part of our nature.

It is best expressed, and most often seen
In enlightened Buddhist Masters.
Trust innocence: wherever
And in whoever and in
Whatever you may find
It, including, of
Course, in
Yourself.

Trouble

It's easy to get yourself into trouble,
But it isn't always so easy to get out of it.
It doesn't take much time or money to get married,
But it takes more of both to get divorced.

It's easy to miss the center of things,
And to get out of touch with
The core of existence.
It's always harder to
Be perfectly aware;
Harder, but not at
All impossible.

You tell me, which is really easier or harder,
To be happy or to be unhappy?

It's hard to be happy,
But isn't it harder still
To live without happiness?

It's easy to be unhappy,
But isn't it even easier
To experience happiness?

Which would you rather take,
The hard way that leads to happiness,
Or the easy way that leads to unhappiness?

The choice is yours:
The choice of whether
Or not to practice yoga.

Puzzles

God is a jigsaw puzzle;
Which part are you?
In this moment, in this life,
This time around the wheel,
Where do you fit in?

The problem that most people have with
Solving jigsaw puzzles is that they
Puzzle over them for much too long;
Or they try to force the pieces to fit in
Where they clearly won't, simply
Because they are too impatient.

God is a jigsaw puzzle;
Which part are you?
Where do you fit in
This time around?

Don't puzzle over this question
For too long.
Act now!
That's where you fit in!

Three Things

There are really only three important
Things to remember in life:
To care, to share, and to be fair.
This is not a new idea at all,
And yet, observing how most people live
Their lives, you might think that it was.

To care, to share and to be fair;
That's really all it takes to be happy.
Share the way,
Tell others about enlightenment.

Care, but don't be pushy!
Don't preach about enlightenment to people who
Don't really want to hear about it!

Share the way by being a good example;
Care by only showing those few
Who express interest.

And, of course, be fair:
Don't present your version of the truth to others.
Lose your ulterior motives!
Be accurate and pure in your presentation of the way,
And you will become the way.

Care, share and be fair,
To others and to yourself,
And you will quickly transcend
Both winning and losing in life.

Beyond

Just beyond your mind's knowing
Is perfection;
It hovers there, awaiting your discovery.
Look within yourself.
Meditate:
Quiet and then stop your thoughts,
Sit absorbed in that stillness,
Wait and be patient,
Just wait,
Because beyond your mind's
Knowing, perfection is also waiting.
Be still,
Be absorbed in meditation,
Wait in light.

Give It Up!

Give it up!
Give it up!
Give it up!
And dance alone.

When you dance with another,
You dance by yourself,
But when you dance alone,
You dance with the perfect partner.

What better partner to match
Your step with than nothingness?
Give it up!
Give it up!
Give it up!
And dance alone.

Completion

There is no such thing as completion;
These are only stages in an endless progression.
There are no final outcomes or decisions,
Since nothing ever stays the same.

Yoga is the pathway to enlightenment:
It is a way of reaching the
Highest stages of awareness.
But, in reality, there is no end to yoga.
Nirvana is not a final outcome;
It is ecstasy and bliss without end!

The flood of light is overwhelming
When it finally comes;
Just as a rainstorm that rages for days
Can be overwhelming.

The river floods over its banks,
Creating a new river and new banks.
And the journey of life changes shape;
It reaches flood stage, and yet it stays
The same.

That's really it,
Isn't it?
Not that there is just one
"It," of course,
Flood stage,
New banks,
A new level in the game of life
In which your awareness is
Expanded forever
Into forever,
Forever;
Enlightenment,
That is.

Be at peace...
It will all work out...
There is no final outcome,
No decision is really definite,
It just appears to be that way today.

The river appears to be constant,
Until one day the rains come
And come and come
And flood stage
Is reached
Forever.

Be happy,
You live forever,
You cannot die,
You can only change form.

Death is a rainstorm;
Birth, a flooding into life.
Nirvana is the sky that the clouds pass
Through on their way between
Here and there,
Heaven and earth,
Nowhere and eternity,
Enlightenment and illusion,
Nothingness and everythingness.

Be still,
Be joyous,
Celebrate creation, preservation
And destruction;
For these are the seasons of your life:
Of your knowing and being.

Meditate
And come to know this,
And so much more!
And oh,
The places you will go,
The wonders you will see,
And the ecstasy you will become!

Trust life!
Trust!
Trust!